Building a Better Community: Lessons from Lemonade Stands and More!

Book 3 of the My First Finance Coloring Book Series

Written by: Ben Hofstetter and Nick Zehrung

TABLE OF CONTENTS

Part 1:

The Lemonade Stand Adventure: Learning About Business and Helping Others

For Parents

Key Themes Explored in this chapter:

- Providing value to the community can generate income, as shown through the establishment of a lemonade stand.

- How to identify a need or way to add value within your community, as shown through selling cool lemonade on a hot summer's day.

- The basics of investing in yourself, as shown through using money earned by doing chores to fund the start-up costs of a lemonade stand. This is then shown again through re-investing earned income into the lemonade stand.

Previously we've talked about bringing value within your own home, but now it's time to talk about bringing value to your whole community!

Lemonade stands are a great way to provide something cool for your neighbors to drink on a hot summer's day!

The first step is to buy the supplies to make lemonade! We'll have to use the money we earned from doing chores for our family and friends!

When we spend our hard-earned money to make our community better, it's called an investment! We'll talk more about this concept later.

The next step is to make our product - lemonade! We'll use lemons, sugar, and water to make a yummy drink!

You always want to make sure it tastes great and is super fresh before we share it with our community!

The next step is to let people know about your lemonade stand! You can create colorful posters and flyers to advertise your stand in your neighborhood!

This is a concept called advertising, and it's how you find customers to buy your lemonade!

Now it's time to set up your stand in a busy area with a table, cups, and a pitcher of lemonade. Don't forget to put up a sign with the price and what you're selling!

Picking a good location and having all the supplies ready is very important for the success of the lemonade stand!

Now we're open for business and customers are thirsty! Greet all of your customers like they are your best friend and be polite to everyone that stops by!

The best way to sell anything is to be a genuinely nice person to all of your customers! Remember, no one likes to buy lemonade from a jerk!

As customers buy your lemonade, make sure to keep track of how much money you're making!

Think back to our discussion on budgeting in a previous book, knowing your income is the first thing you need to create a budget for the lemonade stand!

Now that you have money, it's time to decide what to do with it! Maybe you can use the money to make your lemonade stand even better, like upgrading to a pirate theme!

This is called re-investing and it's the same as the investing we learned about earlier, only instead of using money you earned from doing chores, you'll use money you earned from selling lemonade! How cool is that?!

As you gain experience you might start to think of other ways to provide benefit and value to your community! Maybe you can mow your neighbors lawn, or start a car wash!

Once you learn how to provide value to your community the possibilities become endless!

Part 2:

The Lawn Mowing Adventure: Investing in Your Friend's Business

For Parents

Key Themes Explored in this chapter:

- This chapter explores early concepts of individual stock investing through the lens of investing in a friend's lawn care business.

- The importance of doing research before any investment is discussed by showing some questions to ask the friend about their lawn care business.

- A basic concept of interest payments is discussed in the context of a loan repayment for start-up costs for the friends lawn care business.

Bringing value to your community can take many forms. In this chapter we'll explore supporting your friends and neighbors by investing in their businesses!

Imagine your friend starting a lawn mowing business. Buying a lawn mower and gas to make it work is expensive! You can be a supportive friend, and make a good business decision, by investing in your friend's business so they can afford those costs!

Unlike investing in your own lemonade stand, investing in a friend's business is a great way to potentially make money without doing work yourself! This is because your friend spends their time running the business, and you make a portion of their profit!

Talk to your friend about their business plans and how they will use the money you invest. It's important to understand how they plan to make their lawn mowing business successful.

Make sure you know how they plan to use your money to make more money, so that your investment makes money sense!

As your friend starts their business, you can see firsthand how their hard work and dedication can pay off. It's exciting to be a part of their journey and watch their business grow!

When your friend's business makes money, they might start paying you back, and you could even make more money from your investment!

There are different ways to agree on this with your friend, and we'll learn about them soon. Just remember, always make a clear agreement and write it down before investing!

One of the ways you can make money on a business investment is through interest. Interest is like a special thank you gift for lending your money, where your friend pays you a little extra on top of the amount you invested.

We'll show an example scenario on the next page! We'll also explore more advanced ways of earning money on business investments in a different book series!

Example of Interest: Let's say you and your friend agree to a $1 a week interest payment. If you invest $10 with your friend, and you both agree that he will pay you back $1 each week for 10 weeks, your friend will actually give you $2 every week.

This is because he needs to pay back the $10 you lent him and an extra $1 as a way of saying thank you. In the end, you will have earned $10 extra without having to do any extra work!

Investing in your friend's business can inspire you to think of other ways to provide value to your community!

Maybe you'll come up with your own business idea or find other friends who need support in their business goals! The possibilities are endless!

When you see your friend's lawn mowing business doing really well, it makes you feel so happy and proud. You should feel great knowing that you helped them succeed by giving them the money they needed to start their business!

Remember, supporting others' businesses through investments is a great way to be a supportive friend and contribute to your community's growth, while still making some money for yourself!

Part 3:

The Lemonade Fund: Unlocking the Magic of Mutual Funds for Young Investors

For Parents

Key Themes Explored in this chapter:

- How to understand a mutual fund, explored through the concept of a class of kids investing in a series of lemonade stands.

- Why mutual funds may rise in value, even though individual stocks may drop; explored through the individual performance of lemonade stands within the mutual fund.

- Highlighting the benefits of patience and resilience in mutual fund investing to show that the long term outlook is a stronger position than a short term gain or loss.

Last chapter we discussed investing in one friend's business, but in this chapter we'll learn how to invest in many businesses at the same time! And good news, it's even easier to do in real life!

We can do this by investing in something called mutual funds, which is where many people invest together into many different businesses!

Let's imagine your school and three kids who have their own lemonade stands.

Imagine your whole class, including your teacher and 20 other kids. What if everyone brings in $5 to give to the teacher? Now the teacher has $100 to invest for the class!

Your teacher will use that $100 to invest in three lemonade stands. They'll decide how much money to put in each stand based on how likely they think it will be successful. Here's an example:

a) Stand 1: $30 b) Stand 2: $50 c) Stand 3: $20

After a few weeks, your teacher will update you on how your investment is doing.

Remember, you contributed $5, but because you joined with the rest of your class, you invested in three different businesses!

Your teacher tells you that the class's investment is now worth $120! It might seem confusing at first when they show you the value of each lemonade stand:
a) Stand 1: $30 b) Stand 2: $40 c) Stand 3: $50

We'll see how this makes sense on the next page!

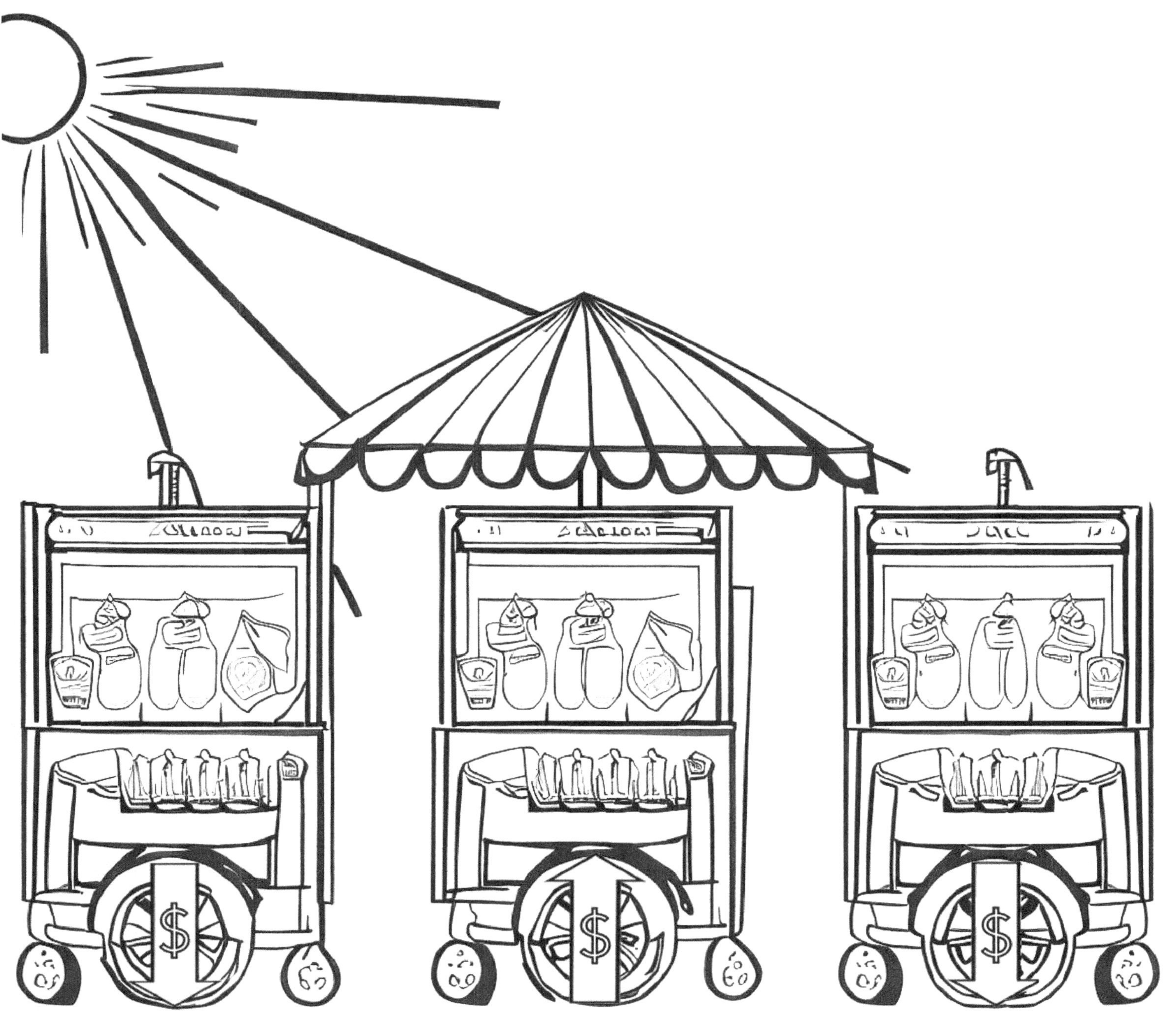

This shows the power of investing in mutual funds! One stand went up, and the other two went down, but overall, the class's value increased by $20!

Let's explain this using a simple example. Stands 1 and 3 are on the west side of town, while stand 2 is on the east side. On a busy day, there was a storm on the west side, so stands 1 and 3 couldn't open. People from the west side still wanted lemonade, so they went to stand 2. This made stand 2 more valuable because more people wanted it, and stands 1 and 3 less valuable because less people wanted them!

If you wanted to get your money back now, you would get your $5 back, plus an additional $1! That's because the class's value increased by $20. Since there were 20 students who invested, the extra money is divided equally among them.

Remember, all investments have risks. Sometimes the value goes down instead of up, and you might lose money.

On the next page we'll see why we shouldn't get scared when this happens, and we should leave our money invested!

A very important thing to know is that investing works in waves! Sometimes our investments look like they lose money, but as long as we don't attempt to turn our investments into cash, they'll eventually go back up! Just like a wave!

Thank you for joining us on this adventure in Book 1 of the "My First Finance Coloring Book" series!

We hope you loved learning about personal finance and wish to continue on the journey towards financial literacy with us.

The next step is Book 4: "Community Heroes and Curious Explorers: Investing With Time, Education, and the Power of Positive Impact!" which is now available on Amazon along with the rest of the coloring book series!

We also have a 3 book illustrated series available on Amazon for more advanced learners. It covers many of the same topics that are covered throughout the coloring book series, but at a more detailed level! The first book is titled "Money Magic: A Kid's Book Exploring Earning, Saving, and Budgeting While Having Fun!"

If you wish to support us and our goal to bring financial literacy to the next generation, there's two easy steps.

1) Follow us on Instagram @myfirstfinancebook
2) Leave a review on Amazon so others can find us too!
3) Reach out with questions at
 https://www.myfirstfinancebook.com

Thank you again for coloring your way through this book and we hope to see you soon! - The Authors

www.ingramcontent.com/pod-product-compliance
Lightning Source LLC
Chambersburg PA
CBHW080341030726
47595CB00012B/4095